down at max's

peter crowley

www.farwestpress.com

First Edition

ISBN 979-8-9887354-0-3

Printed in the United States of America

Cover Artwork by Shari Edmands

INTRODUCTION

My name is Peter Crowley, a rather common name for a not so ordinary boy. I am 81 years old and have never lived in Crowley Castle, though the castle has a place in my story. I've been the dishwasher and the CEO; the laborer and the entrepreneur. I've lived in Vermont, NYC, Frisco, Tijuana, L.A., and London. Now I live alone, though that's not always been the case.

I've had girlfriends, boyfriends, and boygirlfriends. With any luck, I'll have another, though my luck has been more solitary in recent years. I dislike work, typing, and television. I'm content with enabling the creative work of others.

Like Johnny Thunders, I've taken little shit from anybody, but he was the winner in that contest. My story, though perhaps unbelievable, is mostly true. The most fantastic bits are likely to be factual; the mundane, illusionary. Hope you enjoy reading my tales of woe and glory half as much as I loved living them, so here we go ...

Ride Out the Madness
Part 1:

Mr. Jim had walked out on me and married a guy who did political campaigns (one of those people who get 10% of everything spent on radio and TV and all that sort of stuff. What an incentive to waste money). But this guy made big bucks by putting a very conservative, not too bright ex-policeman in as Mayor of San Francisco. That didn't work out very well. He made a fortune in the process and then apologized to the gay community for having done it ... and that's basically what got Harvey Milk killed.

Jimmy was gone, so I came back to New York by myself. I walked into the 82 Club because I saw Wayne County playing there. I had never known Ms. County as a rock singer. I'd seen Wayne only in plays. Both Jimmy and his brother, Tommy, had been in Wayne's most successful play called *World - A Birth of a Nation*. Tommy played a policeman. Cherry Vanilla was in that play as well. It was like an all-star aggregation.

I saw the show listed in the Village Voice. It said Wayne County at 82 Club. I thought I'd go and say hi to Wayne. And it was a terrific band. Marc Bell (now Marky Ramone) was the drummer. An all-star band. None of Wayne's bands were second rate. I mean, he had Jerry Nolan in his band before Jerry was a New York Doll. Wayne had the cream of the crop. His bands were always great.

At the 82 Club, I went backstage just to say hi and tell Wayne "great show" and all that. And he was talking with Leee Childers about the fact that he hadn't made any arrangement about being paid. He wasn't sure what to do. So I just piped up and said, "I'll go collect your money for you."

Peter Petrillo was the owner of the 82 Club. So I said, "It's going to be whatever Peter gives me because you didn't make a contract or any arrangements." Wayne had already done the show so it was a little too late to negotiate. And Wayne said okay.

I went back and Peter Petrillo was not well. But he was in his office. He didn't look real good. He had handed me an envelope and I said thank you... went back and handed it to Wayne. He counted it. It was $500 which was quite a reasonable fee for that time. Then I said, "Don't you have any management?"

Wayne said, "Well, you know, I was hooked up with Mainman, but they just dumped me." And I got some of the details of that whole thing.

I said, "Well, if you'd like I'll give it a try."

Wayne had a reputation as a brilliant, but completely mad artist. There wasn't a line of people wanting to take him on as a client. I said I would do it. He needed somebody to do it. So I said I'll do it.

I figured the first thing to do was to get some shows organized. He had one more already booked. It was at the Little Hippodrome. A club that probably folded within a few days after Wayne's show.

I had been in California so I didn't know a lot of what was going on. I knew that the New York Dolls had played at the Little Hippodrome. It was on the circuit as it were. Nearly every other place was only booking cover bands or had gone out of business in some way or another. Like the Mercer Arts Center that fell down. That was the most famous historical spot where they had all played... New York Dolls, Wayne County, Eric Emerson, Suicide, and Ruby and the Rednecks.

As soon as the Little Hippodrome closed, Hilly had the only club in Manhattan booking unsigned original bands. Of course, I went to Hilly, but he put me off. Told me to come back in two weeks. And I did that a couple of times. And he kept telling me to come back in two weeks. I couldn't figure that out. Because aside from the New York Dolls, Wayne County was the most popular act in New York at that time.

Wayne County was among the first, if not the absolute first, band to play at CBGB's. Even before the place was named CBGB's. It was just Hilly's bar.

I went to Wayne and asked, "Why is Hilly giving me the runaround here?"

Wayne replied, "I was down at CBGB's to see the Ramones and Hilly asked if I wanted to play and I said I'd get back to him ... but I never did."

Okay, so Hilly was feeling disrespected or something or whatever. And I needed a place for Wayne to play. So I went to a friend of mine, Mike Umbers. And I asked him if he knew a bar where I could put on a show. He took me up to 23rd Street to a failed gay bar called Mother's. There were maybe two customers in the place and the owner and the bartender. That was it.

We came in and Mike said to the owner, "This is Peter Crowley and he's going to put on shows here."

They were supposed to build a stage for me. They had a tiny stage where they would have, you know, gay lip syncing individuals work on it, but it was not big enough for a band. I advertised the show but they didn't build the stage. I had to go to the lumberyard and build the stage myself. The owner basically disappeared. We operated with the bartender and a flamboyant gay waiter named Warren.

Mother's had a jukebox packed 90% with disco records, because they wanted that gay bar atmosphere. We opened up with Wayne County for a week. And the opening bands were the Outkids. And another band called The Fast. Both of those bands got the job because they owned a PA system. Wayne didn't own a PA system. Neither did I. And it went very well. I'm not sure if we did a second week right away or if I started bringing in the other local bands.

At that point, I basically raided all of Hilly's bands. I immediately booked the Talking Heads, the Ramones, Blondie, and Mink Deville. The Outkids kind of broke up and the leader came back with a new band called the Victims. And all these bands did pretty well.

Mother's was very small. I began just picking one or two days for each band. Wayne County being one of the very few who could actually pack the place for a full week. At that point, the New York Dolls had gone off to Florida and then they broke up so I never got to offer them a spot at Mother's. But it would have been like a two week run if they had. They had already done that type of gig at Max's Kansas City.

I brought Suicide in. I'm pretty sure the first time I put them on as an opening act for somebody. That did not go over well. And I said to them, "You guys are not an opening act. You're not the sort of thing that would warm up an audience or anything. You have to be the main attraction."

Suicide only had, I don't know, maybe 15 or

20 fans. I booked them for a residency. They played once a week for five or six weeks. And that worked out very well. By the end, they would pack 100 people in Mother's.

Most people thought of Suicide as a performance art kind of thing. I thought they had potential to record.

We moved over to Max's Kansas City when Tommy Dean re-opened it as a disco and that basically didn't work. He did okay, on Friday and Saturday nights. The rest of the week he wasn't doing any business and he asked around for anybody who could help get him back on track. Wayne referred him to me and I went over and I said, "I can do it for you. But you know you're not, you're not going to understand anything I do. And you're not to try to tell me what to do because if you do, I'll just walk away."

So he agreed he'd let me do what I wanted. But at first, he only let me do Sunday, Monday, and Tuesday. He was still doing the disco on Wednesday, Thursday, Friday, and Saturday. That was 1975. Of course, I brought in Wayne to be the DJ on the rock'n'roll nights. Wayne had already done that at Max's Kansas City when Mickey Ruskin was the owner, so that was a natural thing to do.

Then, I brought in all the same bands that were playing at CBGB's. They were all happy to have an alternative. This started at the end of the summer or beginning of the fall of 1975. And it was within a week or two, I was given five days a week. Everything except for Friday and Saturday. Tommy was putting some ads in the Village Voice and we were building up a bit of business. The space upstairs wasn't very big, although it was bigger than the one from Mickey Ruskin's time.

Hilly had done an underground rock festival in the summer of 1975 at CBGB's and I thought that was a pretty good idea. So I decided to do it during spring break. I checked when the colleges were going to be on break at Easter time. Most of them only did one week but they didn't do the same week. You had some of the schools like the week before Easter and the others would have the week after Easter Sunday. I figured that I would do the two weeks, but I didn't have the Friday and Saturday in the middle. So I did my festival Sunday through Thursday. And then Sunday through Thursday again. I called it a Max's Kansas City Easter Rock Festival. We had Wayne County, the Heartbreakers, the Ramones, the Talking Heads, Blondie, Suicide, Pere Ubu, and you know all the ones that became famous. Quite a few of the ones that didn't become famous went over very well.

Directly after that festival, Tommy gave up the disco Friday and Saturdays. I began to have seven days a week and I walked away from Mother's. My mother told me to not burn my bridges, but I never listened. Some kids took it over one of them being that Rockets Red Glare guy who was infamous for being the last person to see Nancy Spungen alive. He was always a suspect in that murder.

At Mother's, he and the others decided to change the name to Zepp's. The place wasn't getting any better. Mother's only lasted a few more weeks. And then Mother's was gone. So, really, then all there was was Max's and CBGB's.

Part 2:

Wayne told me about Mainman and how they had used him to get ideas for David Bowie. And when they were done using him, they dumped him. And I said I'll try. Nobody was lining up to try to manage Wayne County. Wayne County was notoriously crazy. And unmanageable. He remained unmanageable for the entire time I was with him, except that, to some extent, I was able to talk sense into him from time to time.

I was patient enough to sort of ride out the madness when Wayne went out there. Because I knew that he wouldn't stay all the way out there... that eventually he would come back to some sort of businesslike approach to his career. I did the very best I could. I don't think anybody else could have got him a record deal. Nobody else was going to take him to England.

I took Wayne and Greg to England because Leee Childers called up Wayne in New York and said it's all happening here in London. The Heartbreakers were breaking out. The Sex Pistols were on the front page of every newspaper. We had to be there. Otherwise, we would have played in New York until doomsday and gotten nothing more than being famous in New York and Boston. America was hopeless for Wayne County. This was illustrated by our infamous trip to upstate New York. It was not going to go over in Ohio, that's just not going to happen. They loved Wayne in Holland and Germany and France.

They would have loved him in Spain if we'd ever gotten there. They would have loved him in Ireland. We had an offer to do an Irish tour

13

with the Adverts who were then pop stars with a Top 10 song and all that stuff. Unfortunately, the suits at Safari Records refused to give us the money to live on. So we had to turn down the Irish tour.

Better Than a Job

When I was 17 years old, I left home. After a minor row with my parents, I left for the Clyde Beatty Cole Brothers Circus in the summer of 1958. And then I came home in the fall and I quit high school. So when I got home, my mother told me to either get a job or go to school. I said "Going to school sounds better than having a job." So we fixed it so I could go to Marlboro college, even though I had only gone to the 10th grade. And that's a whole 'nother story.

When I took the achievement tests at the end of the fifth grade, and I scored second year college and I asked could I skip one grade? And they said no. At which point I gave up on school altogether. I just said if i'm going to be educated, I'm going to do it myself at home, read whatever books I'm interested in and screw them. I will always get more on the tests because I know more than the teachers. And you know, I was an egotistical little brat. But with good reason.

So, now I'm home from the circus and I got to Marlboro College. And it didn't work. Basically they had psychologically knocked school out of my head and I didn't do well.

A More Rabid Flock

In the spring of 1959, I moved to New York on my own. Various adventures at the time and lots of different jobs. And I went to an anti-nuclear demonstration. In those days in New York, once a year they had a nuclear drill, where everyone had to take shelter in these alleged bomb shelters. They were actually basements of apartment buildings where they had put a 50 gallon drum of water and a sign that said Fallout Shelter. What a dubious, "safe place" to be if they nuked New York.

"Well," we said, "This is bullshit."

We refused to go and we went to City Hall Park instead. And I wasn't there the very first year that there was a demonstration. There were probably 25 or 30 people the first year I was there, I think the second year, and there were about 100 of us out of the 10 million New Yorkers. And we wouldn't go and some of the people there were arrested, not me.

I met all these peace people. An outfit called a Committee for Nonviolent Action. An older pacifist organization called The War Resisters League, which still exists. And they were planning a demonstration that would start in San Francisco and end up in Moscow. And it was called the San Francisco to Moscow Peace walk. I didn't go to San Francisco or walk across America, but when it got to New York, obviously they weren't going to walk out on the water. Though there were some who might have tried. But they got on a plane, the core dozen or so people who were doing the whole thing. They flew to England.

A group of 25 of us decided we would walk from Manhattan to the end of Long Island to take the ferry across to New London, Connecticut, and demonstrate at the Electric Boat Company, where they manufactured the nuclear submarines. Our plan was to take little rowboats and canoes and whatever and get out in front of the launch of this new nuclear submarine and prevent them from launching. Jackie Kennedy was up there with the champagne bottle and we ruined her day because they couldn't do their ceremony until they got us out of the water. We got dragged out of the water by the Coast Guard. And not having that sense to just leave it at that, we went round to the front of the Electric Boat Company and sat down in the road. And then we got arrested for disorderly something or whatever.

During this period, I had met Bishop Itkin. And it's really long and complicated, but he was the Bishop of his own little Catholic Church, which at the time, he called the Free Catholic Church. It was an anarchist, pacifist church. And they had about four members maybe altogether. Nearly everybody in it was clergy. We were at the San Remo bar and we're sitting in this booth and having drinks and he turned to me and he said, "Do you want to be a priest?"

I said, *"Hmmm Yeah, why not?"*

He reached over, put his hands on my head and he said, now you're a priest. Okay. I didn't think much about it. A few days later, he said to me, we really should go through the entire set, even though you're now a priest we should go through the mass, the proper ceremony, and whatnot.

I said, "Okay."

I was malleable at the time. As part of his theology, he had decided that, like in the early church, there should be no difference between priests and bishops and everyone who is a priest should have the same powers as a bishop. The Roman church had divided it into priests and bishops and Archbishops and that all came later a few hundred years after the founding of the church so he said therefore I'm going to consecrate you a bishop.

I said, "Okay."

So I was made a bishop in what's called the Free Catholic Church. He discovered that in England, there was a fascist Catholic church called the Free Catholic Church. And so he decided that that name wouldn't do and changed the name several times over the next few years.

Later on, in the punk rock days, someone around the Max's and CBGB's scene somehow knew that I had gone through this religious thing, but they got it wrong. They were writing a who's who kind of thing for the New York Rocker. Listing each person of note in the punk rock hierarchy with one paragraph explaining who they were. You had Joey Ramone. You had Hilly Krystal. And you had me. But under my name it said: "Former monk whose flock is more rabid now." I was never a monk, but that's that story.

Getting Thrown Out Of Jail

When we were arrested for blocking the road in front of the electric boat company, we went to court. In New London, we were found guilty of something and sentenced to six months in New London's state jail. There were about six boys and four or five girls in the group and, of course, jailed separately. And I say girls, but the women are basically still girls but they were much tougher than we boys. They immediately went on a hunger strike. They weren't gonna eat until they were let out.

The sheriff of the jail told the common criminals, most of whom were in there for drunk driving or petty larceny, that we were a bunch of Communists and they should beat us up. They had a good sense to ask first.

"Are you guys Communists?" they asked.

"No, we're peace poeple," we said.

"Oh you're like kind of religious," they replied.

Rather than going in any detail we said yeah, that's basically where it is. And the ringleader of the local hoodlums said to us, "We knew those bastards were lying."

We're in there about 10 days. The most famous among us was Ed Sanders of the Fugs, one of the earliest punk bands. And he didn't smoke cigarettes. And one of the only things to do was to play cards for cigarettes. One, Ed was obviously a good card player. Two, Ed had no emotional hook up with whether he's gonna win or lose. Therefore, he won all the time. He would end up with cartons of cigarettes, then he would hand them all out. All the guys just smoked for free. So we got along just fine with the "dangerous" criminals in the New London State Jail. We then started teaching them that they had rights. That didn't go over very well with the authorities there. They were very unhappy with having us in their jail and they had not succeeded in getting us beat up . Meanwhile, the girls are on hunger strike. After, I don't know, seven or nine days or so, the sheriff went to the judge and said please get these people out of my jail. And we were evicted. So we got thrown out of jail rather than thrown into jail.

While we were there, Ed also wrote "Poem From Jail." A famous beatnik poem which was a little slim volume but published as such. He wrote it on toilet paper and snuck it out in his underwear - they wouldn't give us real paper. Today, I don't think you can sneak anything in or out of a jail.

But the players of instruments were the Holy Modal Rounders, who became the Fugs by virtue of joining with the vocalists of the Fugs. But the Fugs in the sense that they were were sort of a boy band. They were the much hipper Monkees.

Drag Wanted

In New York, I went and just started hanging out in the street. For a while I was homeless. Ed Sanders worked in a cigar store on 42nd Street and 7th Avenue. I'd stop by there every couple of days, and he'd throw me a couple packs of cigarettes for free. I was sleeping in the movies, it cost a quarter to get in the cheapest of the 24-hour movie theaters. In those days, there was porn on 42nd Street, but it was under the counter with the switchblades, where it belonged. It wasn't out there in your face for tourists and little kids to see or anything. It was subtle. Everything was subtle in those days.

Every now and then I'd be able to get a job. But I'd invariably lose them because I was working for these corporations and they give you an inbox of your day's work. I finished it in an hour and a half. And then what was I going to do the rest of the seven hours that I was supposed to be sitting there? I would take a two hour lunch. Come to work late. Leave early. And the bosses would call me in to their office after two or three weeks of this. They would say we are terribly sorry, your work is perfect, but we have to let you go. Because you're a terrible example for the other people. And then I'd be out on the street again, but with three weeks pay.

We'd go to the Catholic Worker to eat. That is where Ed started publishing *Fuck You: A Magazine of the Arts*. Perhaps the first fanzine. Well, Tuli was already publishing. He was doing *1001 Ways to Live Without Working*. Some of the advice in that book was reasonable, a lot of it was whimsical. He followed it up with a second one that was titled *1001 Ways to Work Without Living*. And that was mostly satirical, but not unreasonable. I knew about this stuff, because I got a job working at the Living Theater on 14th Street and 6th Avenue. This was the actual, pre-hippy Living Theater when they were doing classic bohemian plays. And then most famously, *The Brig* about the Marine Corps and *The Connection* about junkies on the street where some of the junkies were played by actual junkies. And they had a jazz band in the play.

My job was selling poetry books, scripts of the play, and various other kinds of underground literature at a table in the lobby. That's what I did. It didn't last very long because the authorities decided they were going to shut down this subversive organization, the Living Theater. The IRS got them for not paying taxes, whatever. I don't think they were ever very careful about book-keeping, they didn't give a damn about that stuff. It was easy for the government to shut down and get a lien on the property and change the locks. Everybody went in by the fire escape and they did a couple more night plays and the police came and shut that down. That was the end of that era, the Living Theater. Immediately after that they caught "tie dye fever" and started doing these goofy hippie plays and it was not the same thing as highly intelligent bohemian stuff. It was goofy, I thought, so I just drifted away from that.

One day I walked down Macdougal street - Macdougal street and Bleecker Street was the core of beatnik tourist territory. And I noticed in a window of a little coffee shop, a sign, handwritten on a piece of cardboard that said "Drag Wanted." I was staring at it mystified. I hadn't even heard the expression "It's a drag." Yeah, I didn't know anything about Drag Queens or any of that. So all I knew was you would drag a sack across the floors.

What on earth could *drag* possibly mean?

That moment, a young man dressed very mod with a skinny tie and the shark skin suit and all that and the pointy shoes, came walking out of the place.

I said to him, "Excuse me, but could you tell me what that sign means?"

And he said, "Oh, we need somebody to stand out here and drag the tourists inside."

And I said I could do that. So I was hired and he taught me the spiel to use as I stood outside. Beginning virtually at that moment, I stopped shaving and getting haircuts. This is in 1963, early '63. And so I stood out there for a couple of weeks.

"Come on in and see the show. Free admission. No cover."

And then the lady who owned the place fired that guy, turned to me and said you're the new manager. Okay. And she explained what I had as my new duties. As a manager, I would basically make lots of money. Primarily, I would get paid 15% of the gross income each day in cash. Nobody kept any books she and her husband owned it, but her name was Sandy Cropper and she basically ran it herself. She had a best friend named Betty Smyth who had a similar Cafe around the corner. And the both of them had a theory that if you fired and hired a new manager every few weeks, then somehow they would be more on their toes and make you more money.

So, three or four weeks after I became the manager, I got fired. But Betty said you can come over and work in my little coffee house so I wasn't really fired. I just sorta transferred. Then, after four or five weeks with Betty, she'd fire me under this same theory. And Sandy would hire me again. Sandy had two places, one called the Why Not cafe and the other called the Basement Cafe. They were across the street from the famous Cafe Wha. So I bounced back between these two lunatic women for the next few months, maybe almost a year. But I really got fed up with it, as good as it was. There was decent money and all that. The entertainment was fantastic. We got David Crosby and Stephen Stills, Richie Havens, all of whom were unknown at the time. And I decided I would go ask Ed Gordon, who ran a place called the Cafe Rafio around the corner on Bleecker Street because I had heard that he was saner than the rest of them. And he hired me to be the kitchen manager of the Cafe Rafio. Everybody who worked in the Rafio was a Manager, his theory was make everybody the manager. We didn't have anybody to manage. As the kitchen manager, I made the coffee, the sandwiches, I would go to the Italian bakery every day and pick up the pastries and bring them over and all that. I didn't have an assistant or anything, it was a much calmer setting and I didn't have this pressure to make money every day.

How I Became Beard Number 4

Meanwhile, back in the early '60s ... At Cafe Rafio, the manager Ed Gordon was the second person to have long hair and a beard in America. If we don't count religious people. Of the beatnik variety, he's number two. The first long haired guy was a fellow named Maurice. You can find a picture of him if you google, "Maurice, Greenwich Village," or something like that.

Maurice decided not to get haircuts or shave sometime in the 1920s. And he was a character in Greenwich Village. Sold yesterday's newspapers and magazines. He was a famous character. But Ed didn't copy Maurice.

Ed was from New Hampshire and he had been in the Army. Went to Germany in 1945, as part of the occupying forces there and spent two years before he came back to New Hampshire in 1947. One morning, he gets up and goes down to the kitchen where his mother is heating water on the woodstove so he could wash his face and shave . You have to understand the style of life for ordinary people in New Hampshire at that time. You didn't have any central heating. You used your stove. That was what your heating was ... Ed goes to the toilet. He comes out. He looks at his mother. He's got his razor in his hand: "You know what? I'm not shaving anymore." ... and he breaks the razor in half and throws it in the trash.

And then he says, "You know what? I'm not getting haircuts no more neither."

So for the next couple of years, he's still living in New Hampshire. He's got a couple of brothers. Also big tough guys. And every time he'd go into town, he'd get picked on by the local bullies, because he had a beard and long hair and they'd start fights with him, and then he and his brothers would have to beat them up. Eventually, he got kind of tired of that. He decided that he would go to Greenwich Village where he was an artist, a painter. And he ended up operating Cafe Rafio. His partner in Cafe Rafio was momentarily famous or infamous. A fella named Ronnie Von Ehmsen.

Von convinced an older Italian man in the building into leaving his apartment and moving in with his sister in Long Island. The old man came back, furious that he'd been conned out of his apartment for some small amount of money... and he was yelling at Von. When Von turned to walk away from him, the old man shot him in the back, and that was the end of Von. He had copied Eddie with the beard and the hair so they were the first three guys. Then I became number four.

Because as soon as I took that job at the Why Not, I stopped shaving ... getting haircuts. I wanted to fit the public idea of "beatnik" .... and therefore do better at getting the tourists to come into the place.

At Cafe Rafio, we did not do the "drag." Eddie and I would each stand on one side of the doorway; folding our arms in front of us and glaring at the tourists. And then a Clyde would say to his wife, "This must be the real place."

Inside, we'd sell them a cup of coffee for a buck and a half. Put that in perspective. Coffee at the Automat was a nickel at the time. We were Starbucks before Starbucks. Long before there was ever a Starbucks.

One day we're standing out there. The place

isn't even open yet. We're just hanging out and getting ready to open. I had already made the coffee. Eddie and I are standing out there talking about this and that. And up the street came a little short, paunchy guy in a kind of rumpled suit. He was with a real tall, geeky looking guy with long hair (but no beard) carrying a shopping bag. Little guy asks, "Can my client audition for you guys?" Eddie and I looked at each other.

"Yeah, go ahead," we said.

The two of them go inside. We expected nothing. So we didn't even go in to listen to the audition. We're still standing out on the sidewalk. Two or three minutes later, out the door flows. Nelson, Eddy, and Jeanette MacDonald. Both parts sung perfectly. Who was this? Tiny Tim! Unfortunately, he became famous for "Tiptoe through the Tulips, "which is one of his sillier songs. People don't realize what a genius talent he was. He could do Jerry Lee Lewis. He could do Jeanette McDonald. It was absolutely amazing.

Turning on the Cops

By 1964, Ed Koch had become the Greenwich Village district leader. His primary campaign promise had been to clean up the mess on MacDougal Street. So at first, he tried to send the police in to harass the coffee houses. But they really weren't doing anything illegal. They were just selling coffee at outrageous prices. It wasn't against the law. They didn't have cabaret licenses, but that was only questionable legality. He didn't get anywhere with that.

He came up with the idea of having the riot squad on horseback. The tactical patrol force, or TPF, was not there to harass us. They were there to harass the tourists. Pull them over. Ask them for ID. Just generally be a pain in the neck. And that worked. The word got out: "Don't go there, you'll just be bothered." ... and all of our business went in the dumper. Within a matter of a few weeks, there were no more beatnik coffee houses. On the block, only the Cafe Wha and Gaslight survived. The Nite Owl hung in there, but everybody else was done. Koch also went after the strip clubs. There used to be a whole row of strip clubs on West Third Street. And they managed to shut them all down. So Cafe Rafio just went out of business and I went to work at the Basement Cafe.

One night, I'm standing outside the Basement. It's midnight, maybe one o'clock in the morning. There's no business happening. Just nothing happening. The tourists had pretty much disappeared. A young, uniformed cop approaches. He's about the same age as me at the time, 24.

He comes over to us and goes, "Excuse me, fellas, can I ask you a question?"

"Knock yourself out," we replied.

He said, "How come you guys are always smiling and laughing all the time?"

I wasn't going to tell him ... Eddie turns to me and says, "Can I take him in the kitchen?"

"Okay." I say, but I'm not in on any of this. I'm staying out there on the sidewalk.

Five minutes later, they come out of the kitchen. The cop has the first-time giggles and could not stop laughing. An elderly Italian lady on the top floor is annoyed by the noise of this cop laughing. She pours a cup of water down and just misses him by an inch. He steps back, pulls up out his pistol and points it up at her. She ducks back inside and slams the window closed. He didn't intend to shoot. He's just laughing and laughing..

So, anyway, I can't personally claim to have turned on the New York Police Department, but I was a close witness.

24 hours later, the same cop shows up with his brother, also in uniform ... more or less the same age. He says, "Can my brother get some of that?" Eddie says, "Sure." And then they both come out laughing.

Eddie turned on a small portion of the New York Police long before there was any real marijuana movement.

The odd thing about it was Eddie was a staunch conservative. He's from New Hampshire. But he's got long hair, a beard, and dressed entirely in black. I also copied this look. In those days, the only other people that dressed in all black were priests, undertakers, judges, and Johnny Cash.

Eddie wasn't a typical anti-establishment

guy. He was an accomplished painter wearing a *Goldwater for President* badge.

Right around this time, Allen Ginsberg was just starting to grow a beard. And he was friends with us. It didn't bother him that Eddie had a Goldwater button.

Out To San Francisco

I remember Lou Reed, a long, long time ago in an interview said, "My week is the same as your year." Yeah. That was true for all of us. It was just the nature of where we were. At the center of this enormous change in American society. It started really small, and only became a major change with Woodstock.

Anyway, when the authorities finally had managed to put almost all of Greenwich Village out of business, I worked at the Nite Owl for about a week. Then one night, over at Danny Fields' house, I fell asleep and didn't wake up on time to get to work. I woke up, maybe 15 minutes after I was supposed to already be there. I quickly called the Nite Owl and spoke to Joe Marra.

"I could be there in just a few minutes."

"Don't bother," Joe replied. "I'm already making the milkshakes." That was it. I was fired.

In those days, Greenwich Village and North Beach were next door to each other ... with about 3000 miles of nothing in between. There was a little bit of a scene in Hollywood. A little bit in New Orleans. But mostly North Beach, Greenwich Village. But there was nothing happening for me here in New York. The scene in Greenwich Village was dying. I was no longer able to find work and make much about any kind of living.

"I think I'll go to San Francisco."

Green Steaks

It's 1965 and the Greyhound bus was $99 to go all the way across the continent. Three days sleeping on the bus. We hit Rock Springs, Wyoming for a dinner break. We all go to this little cafe to have our dinner and we come back. We're getting on the bus. Just as the bus driver is about to close the pneumatic door, a voice yells, "Wait, wait for me, wait for me."

Down the hill comes this young black man, about my age, running to catch the bus. So he gets on the bus. He looks up and down the aisle. He sees a bunch of old people. Then he spots me as I'm the only other kid on the bus... comes and sits next to me and starts telling me how he ended up running down the street yelling for the bus in all places: Rock Springs, Wyoming!

He'd been on essentially the same bus route 24 hours previously. They had stopped in the same diner for their same dinner. He ordered a steak dinner. And he was tripping. Nobody was tripping in 1965. But this kid was. He's black. He's tripping. He's in Rock Springs, Wyoming. They bring him the steak dinner. The steak is green and kind of swirling. He tells the waitress, my steak is green. I can't eat green steak. The waitress looked at him like he's nuts. She looks at the steak. It looks like a perfectly normal steak.

She said, "Your steak is not green."

And he tells her it is. They're back and forth. Back and forth. The manager calls the cops. The kid gets arrested for "drunk and disorderly." But they didn't charge him with anything. They just put him in the drunk tank overnight. And they very purposely let him out just as the bus was gonna leave. They wanted him out of town.

We hung out the rest of the way to San Francisco and then when I got there I went looking for friends and whatnot to stay with. I had a pocket full of money but I never did find any way to make any more money on that trip in San Francisco. Never got a job or anything like that. But I did go hang out in all the cool places that nobody knew about yet.

Haight Street. The Haight-Ashbury was just a working class neighborhood in 1965. But on the other side of the panhandle, a little extension of Golden Gate Park,was a little cafe called the Blue Unicorn. And that's where "hippie" was born ... and died.

I ended up staying with some friends who were living in the Mission District. Then I lived with another friend who lived way out in Oakland. We came into the city all the time. And we would go to the Fillmore auditorium before it was decorated. It was just this old, empty wooden dancehall and didn't even have a proper stage. It had like a makeshift stage on the far end and the balconies around. Someone had painted a banner ... two stories high behind the stage. This two-story banner had Batman and Robin swinging at you by the ropes. They were holding hands and the bubble said "Make love, Not War." This was how extremely advanced hippies in 1965 San Francisco were.

The bands were Quicksilver Messenger Service. Big Brother and the Holding Company. Jefferson Airplane before Grace Slick. (But I got to see Grace with her brother's band the Great Society at another little venue that had been previously a fire station.)

I went to the Acid Test at Longshoreman's

Hall. I had enough sense not to drink the punch, so I was probably the only person in there who wasn't completely out of my mind. I got to see all this stuff totally by accident, whatever. And I was hanging out with some other kids in the Tenderloin. We would go to a place called the Black Cat Bar. One of the first or the first probably bohemian gay bar. And it was run by a fellow named Jose Sarria. Also known as The Widow Norton.

Down in Mexico

It was at the Black Cat Bar that I met this kid David and his boyfriend. They asked if I wanted to go to Tijuana. They needed somebody to help pay for gas. "Tijuana is in Mexico. Cool. I've never been to Mexico." The three of us went to Tijuana. We rented an apartment together. At that time, Tijuana had rock and roll clubs, one called Mike's and the other called the Blue Note. They featured live Mexican rock and roll bands who were imitating the British Invasion bands. I don't think they realized that the British Invasion bands were imitating Chuck Berry and Little Richard and the way that that whole thing happened was they hadn't heard Chuck Berry but they heard the Rolling Stones. The Beatles and the Rolling Stones were huge in Mexico. But the Mexican groups had translated all the lyrics into Spanish. So there were all these bands. None of these bands sung in English. They would make up their own lyrics to these songs, whatever. We didn't go to Mike's because a lot of American drunks were there. It was trouble. We hung out at the Blue Note.

We got to know everybody. We got to know the cops on the street because we were these weird Americans who weren't drunken frat boys. That was the stereotype of a typical American idiot. One night a cop told us they were going to raid the rock and roll clubs. The purpose of these raids was to make some money. They would arrest all the Americans and get $25 each for bail, to not be thrown out of the country.

One of the cops came to us and said, "We're going to raid tonight, don't come to the club."

We stood across the street and watched the whole thing go down. It was funny. So that was that. We were having a good time, but my money was running a little low. I still had a couple hundred left. In Mexico, everything was cheap. A pack of cigarettes was a dime. Dinner, a full dinner, 50 cents. We started having parties in our little apartment. We made quite a bit of noise. We had a big stereo with a collection of rock'n'roll records. Mexican teenagers would come to our parties and we'd have a good time. But there was an old lady living upstairs. An American retiree. A Social Security lady who was living there for the purpose of living rich with minimal income. She didn't like us or our parties, et cetera, et cetera. She called the cops and said that we were international drug and jewelry smugglers. Mexico has Napoleonic law. Meaning if you're suspected or charged, or whatever with anything, you go to prison. And then they sort it out. You're guilty until you prove yourself innocent. (Pretty much true in America too, but we pretend to be the opposite.)

So, there we are. We're in the Tijuana jail. And they called in the FBI to run a background check in America to see if we were international drug smugglers and all this stuff.

The truth was that I did smuggle to make some money. But I was smuggling steaks from the supermarket on the American side to the restaurant next to our apartment building. Because at the time, Mexican beef was tough. And their primary customers were American tourists who expected American quality steaks. And it was illegal to bring American beef to Mexico.

I would come over with two shopping bags.

The Americans didn't care. I'd give the Mexican custom guy a few bucks and then took the bus into town; delivered the steaks and got a fee for doing this. This was not the kind of thing that the police cared about. It was so totally irrelevant. They wanted to find out if we actually had anything to do with drugs. They did find one bottle of Benzedrine in our apartment. You bought it in the drugstore, over the counter. like aspirin. It was not a prescription drug in Mexico. So that was perfectly legal. There was no marijuana in the apartment or anything like that. But still we had to sit there for 11 days. The good part about being in a Mexican jail was they didn't bother you. They didn't tell you when to go to sleep. They didn't tell you when to wake up. They'd bring food around that was so terrible. If you don't want it, you can send out for anything that you want. Marijuana if you wanted it. Just give them a nickel, they'd bring it back. I didn't indulge in that. But I knew that that was a fact. So, we would send out for takeout. We'd be eating like kings in our cell. There were three cells for foreigners. Only one had a toilet. The other toilets had been destroyed and not replaced. There were dozens of Mexican cells. Their toilets were in perfect running order because Mexican people weren't stupid. American drunks would get locked up. And there was nothing in there to break except the toilet. So, they'd break the toilet. And does it mean anything? Well, first, they're drunk. Second, they're gonna be out the next day when they pay the $25. And they're going back home to San Diego or whatever.

The cops, knowing this, didn't put any drunks in with us. The cell we were in was originally made for one person but had six bunks. Three up one side. Three on the other side. Our cell accommodated 11 people including one older American retired guy with a cane. You're locked up but they don't torture you. And the other folks were these Cuban guys who had tried to sail from Cuba to Miami, but got caught in a storm that blew them over to Mexico. And they were miserable. They did not want to go to Mexico. They wanted to go to the United States. So, they had hitchhiked their way up through Mexico to Tijuana, snuck across the border, and were hitchhiking in the United States.

The Cubans stuck out like sore thumbs. They definitely did not look like Americans in any way. One guy was really tall and had two earrings, a fancy beard, and a mustache. And the others looked, sort of typically Cuban. Whatever that means. They get picked up by the California Highway Patrol who trucked them back to Mexico. When you get thrown out of America and you go to Mexico, first thing you do is spend a few days in jail while the Mexicans decided whether you're okay enough to let out on the street. They wanted to know who you are. Here they were. In the cell with us. We were all well behaved.

Unfortunately, one night, the drunk tank American cells were full of drunk Americans. And they had one more drunk American, so he got put in with us. What does this clown do as soon as the cop turned his back and walked away? He heads for the toilet. Not to use it, but to rip it out of the wall. I grabbed the old man's cane and knocked him out. And I was the champion. God of the cell. In the morning he woke up and got released.

After about 11 days, they called us back out

and we talked to the detectives. They said we all came back completely clean by the FBI and that they were letting us go. The mayor of Tijuana came and apologized to us. They brought the complaining lady back into the cell block. They let her know that you don't make false reports to police and told her if she did it again, she'd be locked up.

From prison, we went right to the drugstore to buy gallons of A-200. The prison mattresses all had lice, naturally. Then, we sent some kids to the haberdashery to buy us clothes and we took the clothes we've worn in the in the jail and throw them in a 50 gallon drum and set them on fire. After a shower and shave, there we were with our brand-new clothes.

The cops said technically they'd have to deport us. Okay. But ... "all you have to do is turn around and come right back in" ... after the various paperwork or whatever at the border. They drove us over to the American side. We then crossed the highway to the other side and walked right back in again. That was my adventure in Tijuana.

Color Sound

From Tijuana I moved to Anaheim. Land of the John Birch Society and Disneyland. I got a job through one of the Mexican kids in Tijuana. He either had a green card or was an American citizen and I'm sure he saved me because I was going broke. I was gonna starve to death. And he got me a job. He lived with his aunt in Anaheim. And he got me a job at a place that made electric golf cars. I don't remember the name of it. But a little factory that was in the shadow of Disneyland.

Yeah.

So, for a few months I made electric golf cars. Talk about Trumpers these days. Everybody I worked with. Workers. Bosses. Everybody there were Bircher crazy, right wing loony goofballs. They thought that I would be upset because I had been put to work on little electric trucks that were similar to golf carts. They were going to be used in the post office in Saigon to get the mail to the troops. So, one of them said, "Haha, we've been making you support the war." and I said, "Why wouldn't I support getting mail to soldiers?".

These people were all deranged and didn't make any sense. They were just as stupid in 1965 as they are today. Totally out of touch with reality, but they somehow thought people who think were anti-American or pro-Russian or some other ridiculous hogwash. They made up those stories about peace demonstrators spitting on the troops coming home. That's all made up. Trumpian style lies. None of the peace people were against the kids who went to war. And the kids that went to war started painting the peace symbol on their helmets. If you don't remember that, that's when the whole shift happened. Didn't stop LBJ or Nixon, however. They kept on killing people. For whatever dubious reason they thought they had.

After working in the electric car factory, I bought myself a car and I would drive into Hollywood to see what was going on. I met some people who were going to build a disco in an old warehouse, right at the eastern end of Sunset Strip. Where Sunset Boulevard ends (or begins).

They were going to build this big disco and hired me to help them build it. So now I had a better job. And one of them had invented something called Color Sound.

Color Sound was a device that picked up the sound waves and divided them into low, mid, and high. And when you heard a low note, it would up the wattage out of one plugin. If you plugged a red light into that one, every bass note would be red. And then the mid range would be blue. A very primitive beginning to a light show. They had hundreds of these devices stacked up in their garage. When it came time to pay me, they didn't have much cash to give me. And I wanted to go back to New York. So, they paid me some cash. Enough that I got a drive away car and enough for gas or whatever to get back to the city. And then they gave me about three or four dozen of these machines. Little solid-state devices were very modern for 1966.

In San Francisco, I'd gone to the Fillmore and watched the light shows. I would go up to the balcony and watch the guys with the overhead projector and how they did it. I brought that knowledge back to New York with these Color

Sound things. The Mothers of Invention had a line in a song about psychedelic dungeons popping up on every street. Making fun of the hippies. I was one of the very earliest if not the earliest builder of psychedelic dungeons. I built one called the Underground, up the street from Cafe Wha. The Underground space is now a comedy club.

This was a place where businesses would open and close. Upstairs had been converted into a kind of Lebanese coffee shop. That failed. And then they turned it into booths, where you could rent a little booth and sell your art, or your jewelry, or whatever. And then the psychedelic dungeon downstairs.

That space was called the Swing Rendezvous in 1963. It was a lesbian bar, but it wasn't anything like you think of a lesbian bar today. The girls, and you're not allowed to say that, were divided into butch lesbians who looked as much like men as they could. Boots, lumberjack shirts, muscles, all that stuff, short haircuts, and what they call lipstick lesbians who look like girls. At the Cafe Why Not, we didn't have ice machines. So, I would buy my ice from these ladies across the street at the Swing Rendezvous. I never had any problem and I'm not hitting on the cute girls because I know that the cute girl's girlfriend is gonna hit me over the head. I knew what was going on here. Every now and then some male tourist would go in there, hit on one of those girls, and find himself flying out the door and then we'd would all point and laugh.

In the same vein, when I was running the Cafe Why Not, the Cafe Rienzi was not a real old Italian coffee house, but a beautiful facsimile that had been built for the tourist trade primarily. My friend Sonny, also known as Sonny the maitre'dyke of the Rienzi. In other words, she would seat people ... working in full drag with a tuxedo. She was only 17 years old so the boy girl thing was impossible to tell. With a boy haircut ... in boy's clothes, she just looked like a boy. One of the things we'd love to do would be ... ha ... I would go over there and we would do a big smooch in the aisle. Totally Hollywood scene for the tourists. We would get a laugh out of that. That's why every day it was exciting and fun playing with these squares all the time.

Old Time Rock 'n Roll

People have asked me how old is rock and roll? I say well, probably right around the time of the Civil War. Mid 19th century. Yeah. And it's some guy on a back porch. Maybe without even an instrument. Maybe with a wire attached to the wall and played with a slide. We don't know and it could have been a woman. We can't know because there was nobody there recording. Yeah.

Let's say I think the oldest rock and roll record is "Pinetop's Boogie Woogie."

The late 1920s is when they first had decent recording. Not good. Decent. That's the oldest rock and roll record.

"You see the girl with a red dress on?"

"Boogie all night long."

Ray Charles stole half that song and got a hit in 1959 with what's essentially the same song.

So, what is what at the end of the day? Who are the Sex Pistols ripping off? My opinion is that Eddie Cochran invented rock. If you listen to the rhythm patterns in Eddie Cochran songs, they're not straight r&b like everybody else's. ... It hits different. So that's rock. Yeah. As opposed to rock 'n roll, but now we're splitting hairs.

London Town

In 1977 London, the punks couldn't figure me out because I had a duck tail hair-cut and a drape coat. I looked like a Teddy Boy. But they all knew who I was. Walking up the King's Road one day and this whole pack of punks are coming right down the middle of the street. They're on their way to the Teddy Boy bar to go beat up the Teddy Boys because the Teddy Boys had attacked one of their friends. The Ted's pub was right next to the tube station I was walking from. This is a mob of angry punk rockers and one of them yells "Let's get him."

But luckily another goes, "No, no, that's Wayne County's manager. He's not one of them."

And then Wayne County and I went to a Teddy Boy show ... Crazy Cavan 'n' the Rhythm Rockers in some old ballroom in North London and again, I'm dressed more like some sort of Teddy Boy. And Wayne's in full drag so we're up in the balcony and a bunch of teenage Teds come walking rapidly towards us and we all think we were about to get beat up. Just then, one of the kids blurts out, "We love your Fuck Off single." (Because it's just a 12 bar blues.)

Leee Childers said look, let's do a tour with the Electric Chairs and Levi & the Rockats. We'll do England and Scotland. (We never got to go to Ireland because the suits at the Safari Records wouldn't give me the money. They ruined everything. But that's a whole other story.)

The Heartbreakers were in London, having been invited by Malcolm McLaren. He had asked for the New York Dolls, but they told Malcolm you can have the Heartbreakers. Malcolm was like many music executives. He changed the name of the band to Johnny Thunders and the Heartbreakers. Terrible mistake, because what was a band now becomes John's backup band. Yeah. Not really, but in the mind of people.

Safari did the same thing to Wayne County. The first album is the Electric Chairs. And the second album is Wayne County and the Electric Chairs. That totally fucked up the dynamic of the band. A four or five people marriage is almost an impossible thing to maintain. And once you make somebody the leader, the king, or whatever, you've destroyed it. It's ruined. It was never Mick Jagger and the Rolling Stones or Ray Davies and the Kinks.

Wayne thinks she came up with the name The Electric Chairs. We actually did it together. We had a meeting to come up with a name. Sitting around the kitchen table, Wayne said, "One the most famous bands in the history of rock and roll has the worst name: The Beatles! Therefore, you can call a band anything. It doesn't matter!" Wayne then said, "Tables, chairs..." and I piped up, "ELECTRIC CHAIRS"... like the Electric Prunes or ELO... So, Wayne and I jointly named the band.

In the beginning, there were four musicians in the Electric Chairs: Wayne, Greg, Val, and a Hungarian boy named Chris Dust ... who was only in the band for a few weeks because they wouldn't let him back into England after we toured the Continent.

The group contract was five equal shares. Me and the four of them. That's it. Now, obviously Wayne is gonna make the most money because Wayne writes the songs. There used to be big money in songwriting revenue before streaming.

Anyway, that's the story of how Safari Records destroyed the Electric Chairs.

In 1977, we all went to Aylesbury to see Iggy with David Bowie on keyboards. Wayne remembers seeing them in London, but we didn't see him in London. We went on a bus. And I think Leee Childers was responsible for renting a fairly large bus and bringing everyone that was part of the New York invasion of London up to Aylesbury to see the show. I threw coins at David. That's how mad I was. I didn't realize he'd saved Iggy's life. Was it absolutely necessary to neuter Iggy? Yes. If David hadn't cooled him off, he would have been dead.

Kings of Rock 'n Roll

The Three Kings of rock'n'roll are:
  Little Richard
  Chuck Berry
  Jerry Lee Lewis

Some people get on my case for including Jerry Lee, because Lewis was an interpreter of other people's stuff. But he was the best at it.

There was no one else better than Elvis, and that's huge praise because Elvis was also fantastic. In the beginning, people thought he was just faking black music. He was not faking it at all. Whenever they played the first couple of Elvis records on the radio in the south, they announced, "Now we're going to play a record by a boy who went to Humes High School."

What they were really saying was, "We're going to play a record by a white boy." They had to be subtle about it. But otherwise, you would have assumed that this was a black person. His genius was he would take very country sounding records and turn them into urban pop records, but he didn't make them sound white. He still sounded black. His songs just sounded slicker. He grew up in the city, in the projects. In some ways, he took country music and and made it urban instead of rural. There was a huge argument of oh, he just ripped off all the black people. First of all, he didn't rip them off. They got the writer credit. Now if their publisher didn't pay, that was not Elvis' fault. No, that was on the publishers.

I was caught in the middle with Elvis in the "Great Elvis Argument" of the mid 1950s.

Because Elvis fans always claimed he was the best in the whole world. And that guy is really good, but he's not the best in the whole wide world.

My mother would say he's the worst. Just absolutely useless and terrible. And by the way, she'd also tell me, "You're playing the wrong Fats." She preferred Fats Waller over Fats Domino. My mother was very hip for an old lady, but you know, her tastes were 1930s and 1940s. And so, I got caught in the middle with that Elvis. No, he's not "the King." But he's really good.

So, is Johnny Rotten, the king of English punk? No, that'd be Johnny Moped. And you'd be surprised by how many people agree with me. Nowhere near that biggest star, but Moped is still the King!

He was real. Real punk rock. The Sex Pistols. Siouxsie and the Banshees. The Clash. They were all upper middle-class posers if you get right down to it, which is not to say they aren't all fabulous. They truly are. But the real punk rockers were the non-college kids. It's like the Beatles and the Stones. Everyone gets that backwards about who was from the streets.

Then there's the bridges between classic rock and punk. Eddie & The Hot Rods. Dr. Feelgood. Count Bishops. Yeah. My favorite of that whole lot is the Count Bishops... not an English band; not an American band; not a Polish band. Zennon LeFleur, the leader, was Polish. The singer was from the USA.

Another multi-national punk band was the Electric Chairs, with two Americans: Vocalist, Wayne County and guitar player, Greg Van Cook. One out of the wilds of Georgia. The other out of Brooklyn. Greg Van Cook. Greg could outplay all three of his idols, Eric Clapton,

Jimmy Page, and Jeff Beck.

When the Electric Chairs played a little dump called the Vortex, Peter Townsend and Keith Moon came to see the show. Townsend came backstage and bowed to Greg and said, "You're 10 times the guitar player I am." That's how good Greg was. And then Greg got kicked in the head. A bar fight. Never could ever play well again. Very sad.

Though Greg couldn't play, Wayne wouldn't fire him. Because Wayne was in love. What do you do with a crazy woman in love? You just have to kind of go with the flow and hope in time she'll come to her senses. So, in the meantime, I brought in Henri Padovani to play rhythm guitar. And if Greg was making horrible noises on his guitar, we would pull him out of the PA and push the rhythm up loud. But that was a very difficult period because those live shows were not good.

Wayne finally realized that Greg was not going to get better. He had lost that ability. Then Wayne said that I could fire him. However, what do you do when the record company tells you can't fire him? They say there's nobody that can do what he does.

There was somebody ... trust me. I called up Eliot Michael in Brooklyn told Eliot, "We need you in England. You have to come over and take Greg's place."

So, Eliot came over. Eliot and Greg were best friends since first grade. And Greg was the first one to take up the guitar. He learned off all the Yardbirds records and played every album better. He would come up with original things and listen to whatever was in that style. And he'd taught Eliot all of it, so when Greg couldn't play anymore, we brought Eliot over.

Eliot told me in 1975 that Greg was the better player. Eliot and Greg had played together in Wayne County and Backstreet Boys. Two brilliant guitar players intertwining with each other. Some people think that Wayne was some sort of goofy drag queen novelty act. No, no, no, no, no. They were right up there with the Dave Clark Five. The Beatles. Everybody. And all those English rock stars knew it. They were there that day. The Davies brothers (Kinks) came to see the Chairs, as they understood the Electric Chairs were on their level.

And of course, the record company suits came to the first show with Elliot. So, the Safari guys went "Oh, it's just as good as with Greg." Well, almost. So close that if you didn't have really brilliant ears, you would say yeah, he's just as good as Greg. He was. He became better over time. For one thing, he got sober. That helped a lot.

Funeral for The Hippie

Back in 1967, I finished building psychedelic dungeons as that business basically dwindled away. I moved back to San Francisco. Me and my friend Carl put our motorcycles on a trailer and got a drive-away car to go to California. We ended up managing a hotel and two apartment houses in the Haight Ashbury during the summer of love. The fellow who had bought the buildings was this hippie guy who had met this hippie girl in Golden Gate Park and they'd fallen in love. Blah, blah, blah. They're gonna get married. Yada, yada, yada. He didn't know at the time that she was some kind of heiress. And for a wedding present, her parents gave him a quarter of a million dollars so he could go out and make it ... "on his own."

It's the myth of the American class system. Those people really believe they made it on their own without a wedding present of a quarter of a million dollars. And we can believe that myth. Well, you could do it because I did. I don't have money for the rent, but you're telling me that you know I can do it. Thinking anybody can be a millionaire is a bunch of baloney. First you have to start out as a thousandaire.

Anyway, he had decided to invest this money and bought these three buildings, including a place called the Jeffrey Haight hotel. My friend Carl and I got to be the managers. We brought in Sonny, the maitre dyke. And so that brings us from 1964 up to 1967. Sonny was brought to be the desk clerk, check people in, all that kind of stuff. She got a room at the hotel for working there. And we ran these two apartment buildings.

When these hippie kids come to San Francisco, it's the summer of love. These records are on the radio talking about "if you're going to San Francisco wear some flowers in your hair." And songs about "warm San Franciscan nights." Yeah, very obviously sung by someone who had never been to San Francisco because there's no such thing as a "warm San Franciscan night." These kids would show up in shorts and a T shirt in the daytime and it was 78 degrees. They were perfectly happy. And then the fog would come in. Then they would be looking for somewhere to live. We were packing a dozen hippies into one hotel room. They were sleeping in shifts. Played hell on the plumbing. I was constantly fixing toilets. And that was due to fact 12 people in each room using the same toilet on each floor. Each room just had a little sink. You had six rooms on each floor. 12 kids in each of the six apartments. That's 72 people using one toilet. I was constantly replacing floaters and all that stuff. Fixing the toilets. And then they had the police riot at the end of that summer. And the funeral for hippie.

The Blue Unicorn was a club in San Francisco since the early 1960s. The people who hung out there were the real hippies. In September 1967, they organized the funeral of hippie. By 1968, Charlie Manson types had moved in. These people were basically just criminals, but could raise their status by growing a beard and long hair. Then they were not just a common criminals, but false prophets. And they preyed on these poor innocent kids coming into town. It was an awful mess. When one of the tenants threatened to burn the building down when we asked for the rent, it was time to move.

The Cosmic Truth

Andy Warhol was friends with us until he got shot. And then he didn't want to know any of us street people. He only wanted to know, rich, famous people. He was scared of us. And he also knew that in the mid 60s I was armed. So that just made him double afraid. He didn't want to know me. But he also didn't want to know Jackie Curtis or any of our crowd any more. And he moved on from Max's pretty much to the Studio 54. So, there's quite a gap. But before I worked at Max's, in 1967 up through 1969, I kept bouncing back and forth between New York and San Francisco during those years.

In 1969 I started a company called Cosmic Truth. And I wanted to spell it like Kozmic Trooth. Like the San Francisco comic book people. My accountant told me you can't do that. Nobody will find in the phonebook. And you definitely could not spell it like that. And I wanted truth to be with two O's. No, they won't be able to find you in the phonebook. There weren't computers or anything. Well, there were computers, but they were the size of buildings. I knew a guy who was a programmer in the early 60s. He had a side job making gun silencers.

Anyway, in the mid 60s, I was armed. I carried a .38 as people were getting mugged in the middle of day because the price of heroin had gone up. And it was just dangerous to be out on the street.

At Cosmic Truth, we sold hash pipes, cigarette papers, and incense. We wouldn't do coke spoons. I understood cocaine. It's for horses, not for men. Watched all these people lose their businesses, their lives, their wives, their husbands, whatever. Because of cocaine. Terrible, terrible mess.

But anyway, we were the only wholesaler of these products in the United States. We had the absolute exclusive. I put a little ad in the back of the Rolling Stone. And I got customers in Iowa and Louisiana and everywhere. Unaware customers would open up a headshop to front for selling marijuana. Yeah. Not the smartest thing to do in Kansas, because of course the cops were immediately right there. If you're gonna sell marijuana, open up a laundromat.

Our business was strictly COD. No credit. No nothing. That first year we were in business we did $240,000. Cash. All from pipes and cigarette papers. I spent all my time either in the swimming pool or in the back room of Max's. I had a bunch of kids working for me. Unfortunately, the girl who handled the cash was Joe Dallesandro's girlfriend.

"Little Joe never gives it away, everybody has to pay and pay."

She was embezzling money, giving it to him for heroin. I was not there every minute like I should have been. Like a hawk. So that was that. Cosmic Truth basically went to Hell.

Lady, Killer

You may know the song Spanish Stroll. It was Mink Deville's only hit.

"Hey, Mr. Jim. I can see the shape you're in. Left hand on your hip. Thinking you're such a lady..."

Now, Willy sings it as ladykiller. But he wrote it as "thinking you're such a lady, killer."

Jimmy was the prettiest boy in New York City. He was the kind of boy who was so fine, when he'd walk by a construction site, the construction workers would whistle. They were not being homophobic. They were just being primitive. Because this kid was the boy that every Roman Senator wanted to marry. But one day, he got mugged in Washington Square. Two o'clock in the afternoon. And I said we're out of here. I couldn't have him getting killed on the street. Nobody's gonna mug me. But you know, this boy looked like a victim waiting to happen. So I tried to move Cosmic Truth to San Francisco. Well, technically to Sausalito. We rented a cool, large house with a four-car garage on the hill overlooking the whole San Francisco Bay. $300 per month.

We used the garage for the business. Unfortunately, the same time we moved there, the owner of HEADGEAR, the company that made the pipes, died of cancer. And his wife just closed down the pipe factory completely. She was only interested in the imported cigarette papers. Those papers made much more money and didn't require any kind of intricate work. Suddenly, my supply was gone. And shortly thereafter, the business just died. This was 1971. We left just before the New York Dolls. So we missed those times in New York. We were in Sausalito, California with a house we couldn't afford, not making any money. And Jimmy's brother moved there too.

"Tommy, they're looking for you, man."

Tommy who was a year younger than Jimmy. He got pressure from the whole family. Don't be like your brother. Be a man and join the Marines. At 17, Tommy joined the Marines and almost instantly discoverd that this was a terrible decision. Doing the whole drill thing. He finished the boot camp. He did okay. He got through it. He's a tough little skinny guy like me, but tougher. One day, he's given the pass to go into town. And he's gone. They were searching for him. They eventually found him and dragged him back to base. He's did some time in the brig, then goes back on whatever duty they had him doing. They gave him another pass to town. He was off ... into the wind again. It worked for him for a few months.

Eventually, the FBI come to my door, wanting to know where's Tommy. I didn't know. I told them to ask his brother, who was making pipes at that moment.

It was a running joke. They would keep hauling him back to the Marines. Finally, the last time they hauled him back in, the Marine Corps told him that they were done with him. Gave him an undesirable discharge Tommy's reaction was, "How could a discharge be undesirable?" That's an oxymoron. And he proceeded to have his undesirable discharge framed on the wall. Now, of course, if you had an undesirable discharge, it's gonna be hard to get a corporate job. But Tommy wasn't gonna work a corporate job. He didn't care. He went and rented a little ranch and started breaking horses. Real wild horses. He also started making jewelry on the side. So he's got these two hustles going and started to make it on his own.

When Jimmy and I went from New York to San Francisco to Sausalito, it all happened at virtually that same time Tommy got his undesirable discharge and was now free. Anyway, Tommy and Fast Floyd, (who at that time, we called Robbie Rock Star) decided to come out to San Francisco. Willy was still in Connecticut or New York. He'd had some bands with Robbie and some without in the 1960s, early 1970s. None of it came to anything in New York or whatever. So, Tommy and Robbie drove out in Jimmy's mother's car. She was buying a new car and gave them her old Chevrolet, which would now be extremely valuable. A Fender vintage bass for Tommy, and vintage Fender guitars from the 50s. That's astronomically valuable now, but back then was just pawnshop cheap. And Tommy had that Ampeg bass amp that you lift the top and turn it upside down, and then you can see all the tubes on top. That amp that all the old blues bands had. So they chose their equipment based on what Muddy Waters' band had. They were totally hip. The reason they were totally hip was me. Because when they were kids, they came to me talking about the Rolling Stones. I talked about Muddy Waters, Chuck Berry. Turned them both on to that music. Willy was probably doing the same thing.

Floyd had a vintage Fender guitar amp and they put these items in the car and head out for San Francisco. But they decide they're going to stop in Chicago and play on Maxwell Street. It's gone now. Gentrified. Tore down all the slums.

All that stuff. But, back then Maxwell Street was all Jewish stores, very cheap, sold primarily to black people. So it'd be similar to 125th Street in New York. And bands would play there. Mostly on the weekends. You'd pay $1 or $2 to the store owner to run an extension cord out to the sidewalk in front of the store. And then you can set your amps up there. Sing through a guitar amp or whatever. There were no PA systems or anything fancy like that. Floyd and Tommy stop at Maxwell Street and they know the routine. They'd never done it before, but they knew what they were supposed to do. So they went to a store owner; paid for the electricity. They plugged in their two amps. And they started playing old blues songs. And they had no trouble making money.

These two kids had the blues down ... as good or better than the Rolling Stones. It was afternoon and they built up a crowd and people were throwing money into the guitar cases and all that stuff. There was a whole bunch of black girls who circled and watched because these were two very pretty rockstar looking white boys who were 20 years old. Maybe 19 years old.

But then Tommy and Robbie noticed, beyond the periphery of all these girls, were a whole bunch of young black men who were not enjoying the proceedings at all. Because these two boys had the attention of all the girls.

So, when the sun began to go down, they thought discretion was the better part of valor. Time to pack up and they got the hell out of there. They put their gear back in their mother's car and head for San Francisco. They arrived in San Francisco shortly after me and Jimmy had arrived in Sausalito. And they immediately wanted to make a band. Jimmy could play a little bit of rhythm guitar but nothing spectacular. Floyd was a really, really good r&b guitar player. Tommy was an excellent bass player. They hooked up with a fellow named Manfred Jones (T.R. Allen Jr.) and I forget the piano player's name but he didn't go to New York with Mink DeVille, who got a new piano player in New York. So, they started playing out as Lazy Ace as the name of the band. I was getting them gigs here and there. Jimmy and I had gotten a job working in a factory that made hashpipes. Jimmy was making roach clips. He was upstairs and I was in the basement of this factory. This was in San Rafael. So we were going every day to work. And I was in the basement. The night shift. Bottling scented oils for hippie stores. Beautiful little old antique looking bottles with a real cork, and a little ribbon and label that said "pure natural raspberry scented oil." It was coming out of a 50 gallon drum that says "artificial raspberry oil." And I got these kids working for me filling these bottles and putting the cork and then we're dipping the bottles in wax seal. These beautiful little bottles. Very profitable. The two guys who owned this factory were two Greek guys. They had the idea to do a shampoo. They were going to go into the shampoo business. They had just enough sense to go there. So I think it was an AARP thing where you get a retired businessman to give you advice for free. You didn't have to pay them. They just did it for something to do in retirement. And they explained to the two Greek guys. Yes, you can do a shampoo. But you need a million dollars for your advertising budget to break in the market. They were able to raise $400,000 and under the influence of cocaine they thought oh, we can do it for $400,000. Of course, the old guys. The old corporate guys knew goddamn well you couldn't do it for $400,000. So, they lost their shirt.

In the meantime, me and Jimmy had jobs there. Tommy got a job there also. Floyd never got a job in his life. Whatever he was doing, his girlfriends took care of him. So they play around San Francisco, Oakland, whatnot. Berkeley too. Jimmy is a gay boy. He was not going to sing about women. He was singing old female blues lyrics about men. This went over pretty well. The gay bars of San Francisco didn't generally have live entertainment. This was a novelty. Here was this gorgeous boy who looked like a rock star with a band that looks like rock stars. And this boy was singing about men. So this was very locally popular and we were able to make some decent money.

Then Willy came to town. And of course he immediately wanted to sing with the band, but he was not gonna sing about men. He wanted to sing about women. This did *not* go over in the gay bars. They did not like Willy because Lazy Ace was not playing sissy gay bars. They were playing in hyper masculine leather jacket gay bars. And at this one bar called the Red Star Saloon, which was downstairs from one of the more notorious bath houses, this guy threw a full bottle of beer at Willy. Tommy put his bass down and me and Tommy chased the guy down down the alley, but he was a faster runner than us and he got away. But we were gonna give him a thumping for throwing that shit at Willy. Lucky it didn't hit anybody.

Then Lazy Ace started to dwindle away. And Willy took Fast Floyd and the piano player;

Tommy and Jimmy just kind of stopped playing much of anything. At this point in time, Tommy had made enough money working in the little factory that he was able to rent a little acreage to make his little horse farm. He got that that thing going as Mink Deville put itself together in San Francisco.

Willy heard about CBGBs on the grapevine and said we're not getting anywhere here in San Francisco. They don't understand our music in San Francisco. They didn't understand it. But CBGB's was a whole nother kettle of fish. Fast Floyd had gotten this girl to buy him an old Cadillac and the dashboard of the Cadillac was all cracked from the ultraviolet. He went to the thrift store bought a ratty old mink coat and cut the good part out of it to glue it on the dashboard. Hence, Mink Deville. That's where the band name comes from. They decided they're going to move back to New York and call themselves Mink Deville.

Willy decided to go to New York. Floyd had warrants in New York for various nefarious criminal activities who knows what it could be. Virtually anything? The line the man is crazy on the coast there ain't no doubt about it. That's Floyd. All my friends were in that song. They got in this ancient old van and they made their way across America. Half starving and whatever. And then you know, they played CBGB's. They played Mother's. I had opened up Mother's. Jimmy and I moved back to New York. I opened up Mother's on 23rd Street across from the Chelsea Hotel. I had to do that because Hilly wouldn't hire Wayne at CBGB's because he was feeling disrespected or some bullshit. He should never have done that because I never would have thought of going into booking bands. If Hilly hadn't done that, there wouldn't have been any competition. Oh well.

Mink DeVille arrived. They played CBGB's. They played Mother's. They played Max's. Nobody understood them. They were not playing punk rock. They were playing 1952 rhythm and blues. With a little dash of Lou Reed. A little dash of Roxy Music. But it's real music. It's not "I hate my mother. Bang, bang bang." They were popular but their popularity was limited to people who knew their shit.

That first Mink Deville album. That album is flawless. Absolutely flawless. 1977 was a hell of a year for albums, including the Electric Chairs, the Sex Pistols, the Damned, the Adverts, the Buzzcocks. But the Mink DeVille album was the best ... though never destined for that level of popularity, even though it did go Top 10 in the UK and Europe. Jack Nietzsche (who produced Cabretta) did a lovely job, but, unfortunately, he and Willy were doing cocaine. And the both of them got more deranged by the minute. And Jack convinced Willy that the band was just a bar band and you need a real band with real studio musicians when they went to make the second album. Manfred got fired. Bass player got fired. Ruben. Ruben wrote one of the great songs on that first album, and they brought in these LA players who could play perfect. But there was no heart and that second album when I heard it, I just thought the band was demoralized ... I didn't know what had happened.

The other mistake was when Capitol Records signed Mink Deville, they didn't sign Mink Deville. They signed Willy. They gave all the money to Willy. This was a terrible, terrible mistake. Now the band was at Willy's mercy. Willy was high on coke. It was all him. The band was still at the recording studio in LA as a band and they're there. They were all there. They were rehearsing. Hadn't recorded anything yet. The LA drummer was a semi famous guy and watched Manfred for five minutes. He turned to Nietzche and asked, "What the fuck am I doing here?"

Manfred was a student of Francis Clay. Francis played with Muddy Waters in the '50s. It was criminal to fire Manfred. Absolutely. Completely insane! Nuts! So I thought okay, he's fucking with the band. They were demoralized. That was why there was no heart in the songs. The magic that was there in that first album is gone. Faded away. So I thought (for many years) it was because the band was just miserable. But then later I talked to Manfred and he said he got fired. He told me what had happened and how Ruben got fired. Willy kept the lead guitar player but everybody else was gone. That album was so disappointing, I just knew it wasn't going to do anything. It had a flat sound. That was the end and, of course, Willy kept playing as as Mink Deville. He even made another album or two with the name.

Then, Willy made some decent recordings as as Willy DeVille. They were always a little too trendy. The production was always trying to keep up with what was popular. That's a big mistake with Willy. You just can't go there. You just let him be Willy. But without the cocaine. When he got cancer and he was dying, somebody gave me his phone number in the hospital. I called him in the hospital. And we had a long conversation when he was near death. And he admitted that he regretted breaking up the band. That was his greatest regret. A little late, but he always had good players. It was the same shit that happened when Mick Jagger made solo records. They're not awful. It's just that Mick is the singer in the Rolling Stones. That's what he's good at. That was a problem for Willy. He needed that band. It wasn't all Willy. It was a real fucking band. Very sad.

Mother's to Max's

Back in New York, the purpose of Mother's was simply to give Wayne a gig. It's a tiny place. So we could sell it out for a week. So I was gonna put Wayne in for a whole week. That was how we started. Opening acts were based on a few simple questions.

Do you own a PA?
Is your music reasonably decent?
Are you a reasonably good live band?
And, did I mention this? Do you own a PA?

I couldn't have Blondie as an opening act until they had one. Blondie probably worked more than any other individual band. They would take virtually any opportunity to play. The smart thing was they were getting essentially dress rehearsals in front of an audience. Working out what worked and what didn't work. Things like that. They weren't very musically proficient. Richard Gottehrer whipped them in the shape when they recorded their first album.

I think Wayne's first opening act was the Out Kids, which broke up and then became the Victims. The Victims were the first band I ever did any recording with. They liked the sound of the Heartbreakers *Live at Max's*, so they figured that I would know what I was doing. I didn't have a fucking clue. But I had an ear and I had a really good engineer.

A good engineer is your key. You do need the producer to guide everybody. To trick good performances out of the band.

At the time, I figured what the heck. I've got it. I've got a venue here. And you know, there's all these other bands and they're all playing. They were coming to me, asking if they could have a gig. I took the Talking Heads, the Ramones, the Heartbreakers, Mink Deville, and the Planets. The Planets were the band that I thought for sure were going to be the ones who would become rock stars in America. They had everything going for them, except a terrible manager. And they got nowhere. Because they had a terrible manager.

For the *Live at CBGB's* record, there were band egos and band manager egos. Hilly wanted the Talking Heads. He wanted Blondie. He wanted Television. All of his stars. He wanted the Ramones. They all turned him down. So he was left with the leftovers. There was not enough good music for a double album.

It should have been a single album. He wasn't rushing out that album. Until he heard that I was making an album.

But I wasn't doing a live album at Max's Kansas City, because we were not set up to do a live album. I had no idea about producing a record or anything. I was winging it completely. I thought to do something live we would have to put in some kind of a remote recording studio thing.

Bobby Orlando was a kid from Yonkers. He later became famous as a disco producer. He wanted to be a record producer. His father had money and he talked his father into building him a studio. He had no background in record producing or any knowledge of engineering or anything like that. But he had a studio. He came to Tommy Dean and he told Tommy that we could use his studio for free if Bobby was the producer. Tommy came to me and asked if this was okay. I said it couldn't hurt to try and we would either like the results or not. We were paying nothing except for the cost of car fare for the band to get there.

The Fast were recorded there. Wayne County was recorded there. John Collins recorded there too. The Fast allowed Bobby Orlando to actually be the producer. He did a reasonably decent job. I thought that those songs were okay. They were usable.

Wayne County went into the studio and immediately pushed Bobby aside. They produced their own record. The Wayne County tracks turned out a little bit weird because he had a new drummer. The bass player had quit and Marky Ramone had gone off to be a Voidoid. And so we had a new drummer and we didn't have a bass player. There's no keyboard player so just guitar, bass, and drums. Elliot and Greg had been the dual guitar players, but Elliott was demoted to bass player. Those three songs are Greg Van Cook on guitar, Elliot on bass, and a boy named Jet Harris on drums. Those three tracks are good. They're not Electric Chairs level. They came out okay and we got three good songs out of it.

The Wayne County Album
No One Can Ever Hear

This recording came after the ESP-Disk album that no one will ever hear. No explaining how that happened. During that time to make a living, I was going around to record stores selling ESP-Disk albums. I was selling wholesale to the record stores, but I didn't have to do a lot of selling. Basically I'd go and check which ones they had sold and would simply replace whatever needed replacing. I'd take down an order and they'd agree to the order and then I'd go around and deliver the albums. ESP was the record company of last resort; the record company of lost causes. The record company that put out albums nobody else would.

I asked Bernard Stollman whether they would like to do a Wayne County album. Wayne County was definitely not going to get a regular record company deal. Bernard was my boss.

Greg and Elliott knew this studio in Brooklyn where we could record and Bernard agreed to pay for the studio. I was a babe in the woods at this time and didn't know you had to get the money upfront. So we went into the studio. Wayne County makes an album The music is commercial. It's balls to the wall, hard rock and roll. The lyrics were as uncommercial as humanly possible.

"If you're in luck and you want to fuck, you can stick it in me."

The album was completed, but was a little bit old fashioned musically speaking. In other words, the Damned hadn't happened yet. The Sex Pistols hadn't happened yet. Both of those added a little edge to the Electric Chairs without copying either of them. But everything became a little more punch him in the face. A little faster. But the ESP-Disk album was a really good rock album.

I brought the tapes to ESP. I played them for Bernard. Bernard was in love with the album, but his fiancee was there in the office listening. She was a massive homophobe and absolutely hated every song. Hated Wayne. He was there and she only saw this mad queen. She told Bernard that he couldn't put out that album. Bernard turned to me and said it sounded too commercial and wasn't going to put it out. All I had was that cassette so I kept the cassette.

Bernard refused to pay for the studio. Now we owed the studio $600. Some small amount of money we didn't have. The studio guy moved lock, stock, and barrel to Alabama ... I don't know, but somewhere down there in the middle of the Bible Belt. I told him to save the tapes and we'd get the money somehow.

We got to England. Wayne and I turned down Miles Copeland who ran IRS Records in favor of going with Safari Records. I gave that cassette to Miles as a kind of a parting gift. Put this out and it will sell. Miles lost the tape. And that was the only copy. The guy that moved down to Louisiana or Alabama or Mississippi had recorded over the two inch tapes because they were expensive. No one will ever hear that album. In a way. It's just as well because it was a little old fashion.

Max's Kansas City, Baby

My whole purpose in putting out the Max's Kansas City compilation was to put out a Wayne County record. Tommy Dean wanted the Fast because he was their manager. I had to fill out the rest of this album. I got three songs. We now had five songs. Two from the Fast. Three from Wayne. For free. Okay, this was good.

Wayne told me I had to put Cherry Vanilla on the record. She was his best friend. I had my doubts because Cherry was kind of a cabaret act. It was not really what we were about. Vanilla said in order to give us two songs, she would need $3,000. I told Tommy she wanted $3,000 and he wrote her a check.

Cherry Vanilla came out of Main Man. David Bowie. The sky's the limit. In the recording studio, you didn't worry about time or money. Except you had to buy lots of cocaine so everybody could be really high while they made the record. They went to Stockbridge, Massachusetts to some fancy fucking studio. They came out with that one song for $3,000. More than the whole rest of the album cost.

Harry Toledo. He had already spent whatever it cost to record that song in his studio. It was really well recorded. "Knots." I heard that over the PA at CBGB's. It sounded really good. I went to the sound man and asked what was that song you're playing. And he told me. So I went directly to Harry and asked if we could have that song for the Max's album. He said absolutely. He understood.

The Max's album was more of a magazine than

it was an LP. A magazine you listened to rather than looked at and read.

I asked Suicide if they could give me two songs for my album and asked how much money they needed. They said their tape recorder was broken and the repair guy wanted 50 bucks. Bingo 50 bucks for two sides. They got their tape recorder repaired and they recorded in the little basement room where they rehearsed. Totally self-produced. Unproduced in a way. Not only did they give me the reel-to-reel tape with the song on it, but they also went up to Times Square where you could record a "happy birthday" song for your mother or whatever. They went to one of those places and had a 45 acetate made. You were only supposed to play those a few times before they wore out. I put it on the jukebox at Max's Kansas. It sounded better as it deteriorated.

John Collins got on there because he was a personal friend of mine and had some really good songs. But they had a fucking band meeting, which they decided that they better save all their best songs for the album. They were sure they were about to get a record deal. They were going to be big and all that stuff. And they gave us an album cut. Not a bad song, but not a hit either. I was pretty furious. But it was good enough for the album.

I heard "Final Solution" on the homemade 45 that Pere Ubu made. I asked if I could have it for the Max's album and they said yes.

This was the end of 1975, beginning of 1976. I was putting this all together. Hilly heard I was doing this album and rushed to do the *Live at CBGB's* album. Never rush, big mistake. Hilly had no ear as you could tell by the bands he picked. They were pretty much all forgettable except for the two Mink Deville songs. The Tough Darts too. He couldn't get The Marbles. I wanted the Marbles, but it was the same deal. Their manager thought they were going to be big stars and didn't need to be on this rinky dink album. Planets. Same thing.

Sorry, we're gonna be big stars. We don't need to be on your little album.

They gave Hilly the same answer.

The Miamis were on the CBGB's and they were not bad, but they weren't their best songs. They had their best songs when they were Queen Elizabeth with Wayne. They were Wayne's band when the band was called Queen Elizabeth. This was when Wayne County first stepped away from doing plays into being a rock and roll singer. They wrote fabulous songs for Wayne, because they understood Wayne. They had a song called "Since You Lost Your Legs."

"I still love you since you lost your legs."

This was completely twisted, fucking insane punk rock before there was anything called punk rock. Definitely punk rock. The Miamis had great songs, but the CBGB's ones are just kind of okay.

We put out the Max's album. The first pressings weren't that great, because the pressing plant wasn't the world's best. How did I find it?

I asked Lenny Kaye who pressed up *Hey Joe/ Piss Factory*. Yeah. He told me about this ancient antique record pressing place in New Jersey that had the pressing machines that were from the 1930s.

The first pressing sounded okay. But it wasn't as good as when the English version on CBS came out. It had a brighter sound and the Italian version. I got the Japanese one. There's a thing called the Thomas Register. It used to be this huge fat book like a dictionary. It had every company that makes anything in the world. So if you want to have something made in Taiwan, you would look in Taiwan and find a place that did wood carving in Taiwan. And that's how I got pipes made in Taiwan that cost me $1.50 that I could sell for for $18. How could you resist that temptation? Of course it ruined America, but that's a whole other story anyway. When I looked up Japanese record companies, I found this one: King Records. They specialized in doing reissues. I wrote him a letter and they answered back with their phone number. I then made a very expensive call to Japan.

And they knew they knew everything about Max's Kansas City because of the New York Dolls and Velvet Underground. They wanted to put out this album even though they didn't know the bands on it. They knew Wayne County, from reputation. We got it issued in Japan. CBS put it out in England and America. Both labels wanted the Fast. Tommy Dean said you had to sign all my bands or you can't have the Fast ... that was the end of the Fast's career. That was it. He blew it for those kids.

Nobody thought that Suicide was a recording act. Everybody thought of them as performance art. When they were in the Mercer Art Center everyone would say they belonged in art galleries and things like that. Nobody thought they were a band in the same sense of anybody else being a band. I thought they were fabulous. And I just saw no reason that they couldn't make good records. They made those two records for me. I didn't have room physically to put both records on, so only "Rocket USA" got on.

The Max's Kansas City album made its way to John Peel. In December 1976, he decided to do a punk rock show on the BBC. It was the first ever, anywhere. And he picked several songs off the Max's LP including "Final Solution" by Pere Ubu. As a result, England was acquainted with Pere Ubu. They began to get write ups. The press discovered the fact that they had these other singles that they had put out. They were invited to tour in England and all this happened because John Peel played a cut from the Max's album.

Now, what did Crocus do? He refused to allow "Final Solution" on the reissue of Max's Kansas City. When I ran into him at the Roundhouse where he was now a star a year or so later in 1977. The first thing he said to me when I walked in the dressing room was, "You owe me money."

That's it. I owed you money? Or you owed me your fucking career? He didn't understand. He thought the Max's Kansas City album was making money for somebody. It might have made a couple of thousand for Tommy, but it didn't make anybody else any money.

Crocus had also lost the two most important players. Peter Laughner had walked out because he couldn't put up with Crocus. Tim Wright ... who produced "Final Solution." ... Who played most of the guitars on Final Solution... Who played the bass on final solution ... Who spent nearly 100 hours mixing "Final Solution" until he got it. This was one of the greatest records ever made by anybody in the whole history of the whole music business. And it is.

Pere Ubu kept putting out pretty good records, but never reached that level of perfection. I knew it the minute I heard it. I didn't know the history of it until Tim Wright told me that he had sat in that studio by himself mixing that record over and over and over until it was polished, perfect. Another record that should have been a hit. Not just a punk rock hit. A hit record.

Tim moved to New York. Peter Laughner moved to New York. But the rest of Pere Ubu stayed in Cleveland. Tim had an apartment in New York, just off Broadway, up near near Columbia University. Somewhere way way up there. And he did DNA. That band sounds like a bunch of racket, but every note is composed and played perfectly in that band. It was the most insane thing I ever observed in my life and I wouldn't have believed what I just wrote, except for when I went to their rehearsal at 171a studios. And I sat there and I watched them. Arto was leading the band. He's playing guitar and every time they'd make a mistake, he'd stop and tell them they hit the wrong note. I was wondering how the fuck could he tell?

It was a holy fucking racket. But I watched him for 45 minutes or an hour. Just stunned that somehow every note that they played was planned as if it was Beethoven. It was the weirdest. The three of them obviously got it. I don't think anybody else got it. People who liked noise liked them, but I don't think anybody else. I don't see how you could hear it as a composition. But then maybe I'm just not that advanced or intelligent. But that's what Tim did. But obviously that didn't make him a living. He smuggled pre-Columbian artifacts out of the Central American jungle into America. Made thousands of dollars doing that. I didn't know about that. I knew "Final Solution," but I didn't know anything about that. He produced a band in the 1990s called Fellini's Basement. They were wonderful. And funny songs. It sounded a lot like a stripped down Velvet Underground.

Never Looked Out for Number One

If you look at the first Electric Chairs album there's a boring, very ordinary picture of four band members on the front cover. On the back, there's a small picture of Wayne in the closet. That fantastic Leee Black Childers photo was meant to be the front cover. Wayne in the closet. He's sitting with the clothes hanging all around, looking completely insane. That was the point here. That was what we're selling. The Safari Records people didn't just not like it. They didn't get it. They thought it was too weird. And refused to make it the front cover. And they put that boring photo on the front, which needed to be on the back small. With Wayne in the closet on the front, (but still not Wayne County &.) The visual tells you Wayne County is the focus. I couldn't get through to these squares. But they were the only record company that offered us anything. So we had no choice.

People have said to me we should have signed here and there. Nobody was asking. It was Wayne. No other record company suits were going to touch Wayne with a 10 foot pole. And no other person was going to manage Wayne but me. And no other record company was going to sign them except Miles Copeland at IRS Records. And he didn't pay royalties. If we went with Miles, we would have had the same problem as the Cramps who had to take him to court to get their money. And he had an injunction that they couldn't put out records for two years or something. It was a horrible mess.

So, I went with Safari Records, which was a slightly less horrible mess. But, after recording

Storm The Gates Of Heaven, the rhythm section of the Electric Chairs decided that I was mean to them. I worked them too hard. I was really the bad manager. Blah. Blah. Blah. And they wanted me out of there. They went to Safari and said, "We want him gone." Each one wanted me gone because I was constantly telling them they needed to do this, that, and the other thing. They didn't notice I was always sticking up for the band. Anyway, between those two packs of fools, the rhythm section and Safari Records, I was told, "If you don't leave, we're taking the band's salary away and we're not going to put out another album."

Wayne heard that they had done this and came to me and said, "Let's go back to New York. Screw these people."

I should have said yeah, let's go back to New York. But I didn't because I never looked out for number one. I told Wayne, "You have a brilliant band. As good as any band on the planet; now or ever. You have a record deal. You should stay and stick it out."

So, I told the suits I'd leave. What else could I do? They asked me how much money I wanted. I said, "Give me $1,500." as that was how much I needed to get back to New York and rent an apartment there. I didn't ask for more because I knew they'd deduct whatever they gave me from the band's royalties. However, my sacrifice was for naught, 'cause they claimed to have given me $15,000... and ultimately stole $13,500 from Wayne!

There was no hope of an American record company picking Wayne up. Wayne was too crazy even for ESP-Disk.

In 1975, I had made a brief deal with ESP-

Disk' Records. Wayne County & The Backstreet Boys recorded an album for them, but then Bernard Stoleman refused to put it out. That'll tell ya the hopelessness of Wayne in New York.

Unfortunately, at the time, I didn't think of the fact that we didn't need a record company. We had Max's Kansas City.

Anyway, I said to Wayne, "You should stay."

The result was LP number three: *Things Your Mother Never Told You*.

That album has two good cuts on it. Both of which are definitely not rock'n'roll: "Berlin" and "Waiting for the Marines," which were also released as a single. The record company guys had the brilliant idea of not putting any information on the label of that single. Nothing but a Berlin postmark. Very hip except you look at the plain sleeve. "What is this?" You'd have to play it and even then you wouldn't know what it was. You couldn't tell who the band was or anything. The record company thought they were really smart. They outsmarted themselves. If it had been in the picture sleeve, or something, that would have been okay. But anyway, they did that.

They hired David Cunningham to be the producer. He was famous for being in the Flying Lizards, which was just him playing all the parts. And he was really good at that type of novelty shit, but that has nothing to do with Wayne County. To this day, Wayne hates all the experimental sounds on that album. No powerful, straight ahead rockers on that album. Production is weedy. It was because you had a producer mixing them who doesn't do rock'n'roll music.

That album actually sold pretty well, because it was trendy. Goofy was selling at the time.

But ultimately, it ended the band. That was it. In the process of these shenanigans with the band members and the record company, Safari got me to sign my way out of the contract and then they talked the entire band and Wayne into a brand new contract. This totally nullified the deal in which we were all equal members. The new contract was Wayne and employees. Ha Ha! Who gets royalties from the Safari Records? Wayne. To this day. Because those fools wanted me gone and didn't realize they were signing away everything in the process. Instant karma got them. They felt stifled playing straight rock'n'roll. They wanted to experiment. They really thought they were the Electric Chairs. They were convinced. They could've come to me and said they wanted to make an experiment album. I would have tried my very best to get the Safari people to agree to it and do it with David Cunningham, with or without Wayne on vocals.

It would have been the band. Could've called it just The Eclectic Chairs or something like that. But they didn't come to me. They didn't talk to me. They didn't complain to me. Nothing. They just went and pulled this stunt.

Wayne didn't just go to Berlin. The band fired Wayne. They were so convinced that they were the Electric Chairs and Wayne was just the vocalist and therefore replaceable that they actually fired Wayne from the Electric Chairs. Safari being only kind of 80% stupid allowed the Electric Chairs without Wayne to record a single. Put this out and see what happens. They recorded a single that was okay for what it is. It sounds like the stuff on *Things Your Mother Never Told You*. I don't even remember if there was a vocal on it. If there is, it was probably Henri.

Anyway, it tanked. And then they had the balls to book themselves at clubs around London as the Electric Chairs with Wayne already fired and gone off to Berlin. So people would buy their tickets and came expecting to see Wayne County and the Electric Chairs. Naturally, you expect to get Wayne County with the Electric Chairs. The band would come out. The first song or two was cool because everybody was expecting that. It was very traditional for the band to play a while and then the star made the grand entrance. Only the star didn't make the grand entrance. And when they realized Wayne wasn't appearing, people threw things. That was the end of the Electric Chairs. It ended before it started. Totally a non-starter. Eliot swears he had nothing to do with the mutiny. I don't know. But he did come back with Wayne and continued to play with Wayne, so probably didn't have anything to do with it. I don't know. I wasn't there.

Wayne got fired and moved to Berlin and had nothing to do with the band anymore. But he still owed Safari one more album.

The First Live Album of the 80s

Now we come to another one of my great mistakes. Wayne came back and the band was gonna do a live album. To fulfill the contract. They made one of the classic live album errors. They picked a particular show to be the live album. You don't pick the live album show until after you had played it. It may sound like crap. They had no guidance. I was gone. I definitely would not had gone along with that. This date was going to be the live album. That's so ridiculous.

You can see by the way I did the Heartbreakers' *Live at Max's Kansas City*. I recorded show after show after show after show in order to get an album.

Wayne's new Electric Chairs went to Canada. They were going to record the very first live album of 1980... It was New Year's Eve 1979 and they would play through midnight. That was the gimmick. The first, very first, live album of the 80s. The problem was that it was no longer the Electric Chairs. It was Elliot from the Electric Chairs. A really good drummer. Johnny or Joey something. And Peter Jordan, the New York Dolls' stand-in bass player, filling in on bass guitar. Unfortunately, Peter got drunk and played like crap through the whole show. Out of tune. The theory became if they took this recording and erased the bass and had Peter, sober, play bass in the studio, it'd fix everything. But it didn't. Because when one player is off, he throws off everybody else. And so the magic didn't happen because the drummer and the guitar player were thrown off by the fact that the bass player was drunk and couldn't play right. They went in the studio and they worked and worked on a 'fix-in-the-mix'... and when they came to me and had me listen to different mixes and whatever, itdidn't fucking dawn on me to say, "Scrap it."

I should have told them that we would record live right here at Max's Kansas City. Forget the live recording in Toronto. It was a failure. We should have booked three days in Max's. Six shows. Played six shows and picked the best out of that. That's what I should have done. That's what I did with the Heartbreakers. Why I didn't think of it at that time with Wayne I don't know. My heart wasn't in it or whatever. You know, I just didn't do it.

When that album came out it was pretty dire. Jimi LaLumia took over as Wayne's manager. On some levels, he did really good job. Publicity was fabulous, but he convinced Wayne to do a disco dance music 12-inch of "Fuck Off," which is the most horrible sounding thing. Embarrassing beyond belief. Jayne hated it. Still hates it. But Jimi LaLumia did a good job otherwise, and got Wayne's royalties for him.

Gordon Sumner's Rorschach Test

Miles Copeland put out the Electric Chair EP that I produced. I also produced two more songs from that session. Although on those two songs it said produced by Miles Copeland and Peter Crowley. The only thing Miles did was put up the money. The single that came out after the success of the EP was remixed by Miles. My production was too raw or too something they didn't like. They made it sound really wimpy it has my name on it which is embarrassing to me.

None of us got a penny out of any of that beside the value of the record coming out. Well, except that Squeeze got enough money together to buy a nice new Ford van and so Miles gave it to us take to Europe. But he didn't tell us it belonged to Squeeze. He said it was his. It wasn't. But he was the manager of Squeeze and therefore he could get away with that sort of thing. It was quid pro quo. The pro was we had to take the Police who would be the opening band.

I didn't get along with Gordon at all.

Everybody got along with Henri and Stewart Copeland. He's a nice nice fella. But Mr. Sumner was an asshole. Now he's a billionaire asshole. Nice guys finish last, what can I say?

Gordon is talented. You gotta give him the fact that he appeals to millions of people. I couldn't stand him. He just drove me right up the wall. And he hates me with a purple passion because I asked him to read the maps.

That was my great sin.

We're going across Holland. I don't read Flemish. So every time there was a crossroads or something where I have to make a choice of which way to go, I had to stop. Get the map out. We didn't have the internet or anything in 1970s. And I had to figure out where we were coming from and none of the streets are in English. So I looked at the sign and then looked for the matching words on the map. Which way to Utrecht? So it was a pain in the ass. I was spending 10 to 15 minutes at each major intersection to go through this business.

Mr. Sumner insisted, always, on having shotgun. He wanted that front seat. Okay, you're in the front seat. I am the driver. Like in a car rally, the person in the passenger seat does the map reading. Back when we had maps. So I asked him to follow along on the map. And when we get to the intersection, Gordon could then tell me which way to go. And that way I wouldn't have to spend 15 minutes pouring over this map to figure out where we were and where we were getting.

Well, you'd have thought I asked him to trim my toenails or shine my shoes or something. He became incredibly irate. He was furious that I would ask "the star" to do this menial work. The mere driver of the van asking me to do this.

What a jerk.

When he wrote his autobiography 35-40 years later, he devoted several pages to insulting me. It was a long and involved thing. The funniest part was when he said that my hair looked like a penis. Now, that doesn't say anything about me, but that says a great deal about Gordon.

Whether it is a Freudian or Jungian point of view, it does reveal something about Gordon. He could have just called me a dick, but whatever. He looked at my hair and saw a penis. This was Gordon Sumner's Rorschach test.

Look at the inkblots. If you see sexual organs in there, this tells the psychiatrists that you've got some kind of hang up. So there it is. He made special care to say nice things about Wayne in this same chapter. You know, Gordon doesn't want to come across like an asshole.

At the time, the Police were completely unknown. Wayne was already known, because of the plays and the earlier things that had happened before his rock and roll career. Wayne was known as a minor celebrity all over Europe. In 1973, Wayne had a huge picture on the cover of Melody Maker, which goes all over, not just England, but all over Europe. And most stories about Andy Warhol would mention Wayne and things like that. He was part of that whole culture which was of interest on the continent.

The people who came to the shows in Holland and in France, particularly in Holland, were all ages. When I say all ages, I mean everyone from 10 to 60. The 12 year old kids were drunk and they with their parents. They were not being allowed out to carry on but they were allowed to have a party. They were falling around. The bad part was that you played these gigs and trays of pints of 10% beer would come into the dressing room. Before you had a chance to take two sips out of the first mug, another tray would come. It was near impossible for me to keep the band members sober enough to play. It didn't much matter because the audience was so fucking drunk. They didn't know.

The Police went over well but Wayne went over a whole lot better. How much of the lyrics did anybody understand? I don't know, probably not much. English as a second language is fairly common but it's not universal.

The second time we went to the continent, we didn't take the Police everywhere with us, but we did team up with the Police in Paris. It was billed as a punk festival. Wayne was the headliner. Generation X with one or two other English bands and then a whole slew of never to be known French punk bands were opening the show. It was at a movie theater that held about 800 people. A medium-size movie theater.

Billy Idol threw a fit because we were asking him to go on before the Police. We really didn't care when he went on in any show biz sense. However, the Police and the Electric Chairs used the same backline. We were not going to move it twice. It was going to be the Police and the Electric Chairs.

Billy was saying, "I am not going on before the Police." I asked Billy, "How would you like to close the show?"

He lit up. He was really happy. "Oh, now I'm the headliner," he thought. Problem solved.

The French bands played. Nobody cared. Police played. The Electric Chairs played. And then 400 of the 800 people in the place leave. Billy played to a half empty house which I knew was gonna happen. He would have been much better off going on before the Police because he wasn't particularly famous. The Police were less famous but neither one of them was in the Electric Chairs category. You can't follow Wayne County. It simply was not possible. Unless you wait a long time.

I remember seeing the Rolling Stones go on after Ike and Tina. They made us wait an hour and 15 minutes. You do not go on right after Ike and Tina. This was 1969. Madison Square Garden. I wouldn't pay money to see the Rolling

Stones. I don't dislike them, but I don't like them that much.

I'm a Muddy Waters fan. To me, the Stones were a second rate Chuck Berry or Muddy Waters. They did come up with some brilliantly derivative but original songs. After the first two cover albums, they came up with Mothers' Little Helper and Satisfaction. That period Rolling Stones I might have paid money to to see. But by 1969, they'd become kind of just a blues band now that Brian was gone. And as good as Mick Taylor is. It was ordinary.

Fuck the Rules

In London, it was not the Electric Chairs yet. We hadn't sat down and tried to come up with a name. It was just Wayne County with backing musicians. The Roxy was little tiny venue. The most important venue in London in late 1976, early 1977... Wayne's opening act was the Adverts.

The Roxy was a tiny club. The stage was miniscule. The Adverts were expected to set up their drum kit in front of our drum kit, leaving no space for the singer to get in front of the drum kit. The other players in the opening act would be to the sides of their drummer. Ridiculous. I said to our drummer that we were moving your drums out of the way so they can set up properly for their shop. This was unheard of. Miles Copeland was yelling at me. You were not supposed to do that. I was doing the right thing. I don't care what the rules were.

Fuck the rules.

The Adverts did their show. Wayne did his show. Both went down really well. Wayne more so, because it was fucking Wayne. Time to get paid. In the dressing room, I got handed the money. It was close to 1,000 pounds. We made really good money on that show. And Michael Dempsey, the manager of the Adverts, was supposed to give me half the cost of the PA. The deal was he'd give me half the cost of the PA and not get paid. So I thought that was as stupid as making people set the drums up in front of the other drums.

I asked Michael, "What did it cost you guys to come here?" And he said, "Well, we had to rent a delivery guy to bring our backline and stuff." About 30 pounds. I said, here's 30 pounds and you do not have to pay for half the PA. (I felt it was a disgusting deal.)

Miles Copeland was standing there and he's really livid, pissed off at me now, and he goes, "You're ruining the system. "

Well, it needed ruining.

At that moment, the Adverts were nobody. They were the band that you would hire to open. I think it was three months, maybe four months later. The Adverts have the number 6 song on the British fucking Hit Parade. "Gary Gilmore's Eyes." They were suddenly headlining big halls. 1,500 seats. It was not 75 or 100 kids at the Roxy. Michael Dempsey called me up and asked us to be on a show. It was the Adverts who got the big letters. Wayne County in smaller letters.

When we get to the venue Michael Dempsey made their drummer move his drums and put ours on the drum riser. This was a big fucking show at the Roundhouse. 1,500 capacity and it was sold out because the Adverts had the number 6 song. The drums had been moved for us, Michael and I went to the sound guy. I gave him some money ... and we explained that there were two headliners. You got two opening acts. You do whatever you normally do with opening acts. And the next two bands are both headliners. They both get 100% of sound. They get 100% of light. We went to the light guys. Same thing.

All because I had spent a measly 30 pounds at the Roxy. This fucking music business has people who are such scumbags. They just don't understand that if you do the right thing. It comes back around.

The Roundhouse's owner came backstage before the first band went on and he laid down the law. He didn't know that we had already told the sound and light people that there were two headliners. So he said the three opening acts would do 30 minutes each ... with no encores!

He left and went back up to the box office in the front. I turned to Wayne and I said write a setlist that's exactly 25 minutes.

I told Wayne to trust me. You're gonna get up there. You're gonna do 25 minutes of your strongest material. And you're going to end with such power there will be an encore. Nobody in the audience knew who they were. Out of the 1,500, there were maybe 50 Electric Chairs fans from the small gigs.

The announcer announces the Electric Chairs. And there's a little applause from 1500 people. A couple of polite people. Nothing welcoming whatsoever. And then it fucking hits. And it was so powerful. At the end of that 25 minutes, the audience was absolutely going crazy. Completely fucking berserk. And the owner, John Curd comes running down the aisle to get to the backstage and he said, "Get them back on. Get them back on. They're destroying my place."

That was it, you see?

You got the fucking damn star, but Wayne never had a manager like that before. Without a manager, who knows if Wayne would have gone beyond being a novelty. His songs were so weird and everything about him was so peculiar. Even today, they would still be peculiar. With me, he had a shot.

The saddest part of this story was Michael Dempsey. He had one of those houses where the second floor is kind of like a balcony over the living room and he fell over, completely drunk. I think it was a week or two after the Roundhouse. He had offered us the tour with the Adverts in Ireland. He fell over and hit his head and died. The Adverts broke up. That was the end of them because they needed him.

If the Rolling Stones didn't have an Andrew Loog Oldham, they would never have been anybody. They would have been another English r&b band. If the Beatles didn't have Brian Epstein, they wouldn't have gotten out of the Gene Vincent leather juvenile delinquent costume. Brian made them look innocent and, and appeal to all the preadolescent girls who made their career. Preadolescent girls don't like boys in black leather. Maybe they do now. I don't know. In that time, it was exactly the right move. Made them look innocent. And nice. Yeah, it was very important.

The manager serves a super important role. Willy Deville had a great manager. He really got the Capitol Records contract. And then Willy and the record company stabbed him in the back. They signed Willy directly. The manager was out.

People don't understand it. A real manager is not some guy who just steals a bunch of money. It is someone who tells you what to do. And who bribes the sound man. Someone who negotiates your gigs. Someone who deals with the nervous breakdown the singer is having. Someone who drives the fucking van. Most people don't understand how important that is.

ALSO OUT ON FAR WEST

farwestpress.com

+1 (541) FAR-WEST